PUFFIN BOOKS
RATTU AND POORIE'S ADVENTURES IN HISTORY: 1857

Parvati Sharma's first book for children, *The Story of Babur*, was acclaimed as 'delightful' and 'deeply engaging'. She has also written books for adults: *The Dead Camel and Other Stories of Love*; *Close to Home*, a novella; and, most recently, *Jahangir: An Intimate Portrait of a Great Mughal*, a historical biography. Sharma lives in New Delhi, where she has studied English literature and Indian history, and worked as a travel writer, editor and journalist.

ADVANCE PRAISE FOR THE BOOK

'This hilarious romp through history will appeal to young and not-so-young readers alike. Humour, imagination and engaging protagonists make this book a delightful read'
—Devika Rangachari, historian and author of *Queen of Ice*

'Parvati Sharma makes a joyous partnership of history and humour, transporting young readers into the presence of the colourful and courageous personalities who led the revolt of 1857. There has never been a more fun way to know history!'
—Arshia Sattar, author of *Ramayana for Children*

ALSO IN PUFFIN BY PARVATI SHARMA

The Story of Babur

Rattu & Poorie's ADVENTURES IN HISTORY 1857

PARVATI SHARMA

Illustrations by Meghna Menon

PUFFIN BOOKS

An imprint of Penguin Random House

PUFFIN BOOKS

USA | Canada | UK | Ireland | Australia
New Zealand | India | South Africa | China

Puffin Books is part of the Penguin Random House group of companies
whose addresses can be found at global.penguinrandomhouse.com

Published by Penguin Random House India Pvt. Ltd
7th Floor, Infinity Tower C, DLF Cyber City,
Gurgaon 122 002, Haryana, India

Penguin
Random House
India

First published in Puffin Books by Penguin Random House India 2019

Text copyright © Parvati Sharma 2019
Illustrations copyright © Meghna Menon 2019

All rights reserved

10 9 8 7 6 5 4 3 2 1

This is a work of fiction. All situations, incidents, dialogue and characters, with the exception of some well-known historical and public figures mentioned in this novel, are products of the author's imagination and are not to be construed as real. They are not intended to depict actual events or people or to change the entirely fictional nature of the work. In all other respects, any resemblance to persons living or dead is entirely coincidental.

ISBN 9780143444374

Typeset in Adobe Caslon Pro
Book design and layout by Parag Chitale
Printed at Aarvee Promotions, India

www.penguin.co.in

For Poorva Rajaram and Ratna Appnender,
with love

LAKSHMI BAI AND JHALKARI BAI

Rattu was in a bad, mad mood. She made a ghastly face at Roundy the cat, and Roundy the cat hid behind the sofa. She made a ghastly face at Shanti the cook, and Shanti the cook hid behind the fridge. She made a ghastly face at Mama on the balcony, and Mama on the balcony hid behind a newspaper. When she had nobody left to make ghastly faces at, Rattu stomped her feet on the floor.

'If you *have* to stomp,' said Mama from behind her newspaper, 'go stomp in your bedroom.'

Rattu went to her bedroom and stomped there for a while, and then she had a better idea. She climbed on to Poorie's bed and began to stomp on that.

Poorie was Rattu's older sister, and Poorie had been horrid and mean.

First of all, it was Rattu who had asked for a bow-and-arrow set for her Pongal gift.

Second of all, it was Poorie who had made fun of Rattu and said, 'Your bow-and-arrow is so stupid.'

And *worst* of all, Poorie had run off with Rattu's bow-and-arrow, to play with *her* friends, and left Rattu all alone.

Rattu stomped on Poorie's bed, then she jumped on it. She kicked at the pillow and bounced on it. She danced on the mattress and made a mess of the sheets. And with every jump and every stomp, and every kick and every leap, she said, 'Take that, Poorie, take *that*, Poorie!'

Finally, when she had no more stomps left in her, Rattu stopped. The bed looked like . . .

a crumpled sheet of paper, and . . .

a chewed-up glob of gum, and . . .

a dog all wet with mud.

Rattu looked at the crumpled, chewed-up, doggy-muddy mess, and she felt quite happy. *It served Poorie right.*

But after she had finished feeling happy, Rattu began to feel a little scared. When Poorie came home, she would be *hopping mad*. And Mama and Papa would be *hopping mad*.

'I wish,' thought Rattu, 'I wish I had a *soldier* on a big horse, with a big sword, who would fight everybody and take my side.'

Just as Rattu made her wish, the bed began to rumble and the room became black. Just as Rattu made her wish, the air began to frizzle and the floor began to crack.

'What's happening?' thought Rattu.

And just as she thought it, two big brown horses climbed up from the cracks in the floor.

The horses looked exactly the same.

There was a soldier on each horse, and the soldiers looked exactly the same. Both soldiers held big swords in their hands, and the swords looked exactly the same.

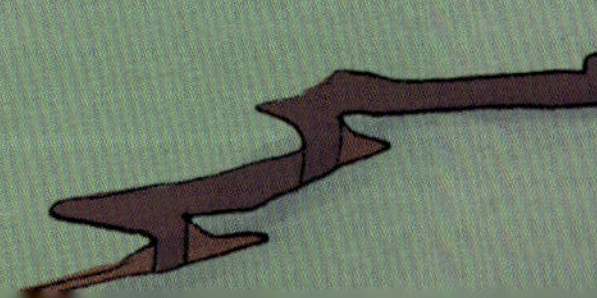

The soldiers waved their swords about, and the swords clanged at the fan.

'Oops,' said the soldiers, in exactly the same voice.

'Who are you?' said Rattu.

'My name is Manikarnika,' said the first soldier, 'and this is my horse, Badal.'

'Oh,' said Rattu.

'Well,' said the first soldier, looking irritated, 'I suppose you have no idea who I am?'

'I *know*,' said Rattu. 'You're the soldier I wished for.'

'Well, *actually . . .*' said the first soldier.

Just then the second soldier spoke up. 'My name is Jhalkari Bai and this is my horse, Bijli. *That*,' she pointed at the first soldier, 'is the rani of Jhansi.'

'No,' said Rattu, 'the rani of Jhansi was called Lakshmi Bai. *She* is called Manikarnika.'

Jhalkari Bai laughed. 'Manikarnika is her *real* name, but Lakshmi Bai is her *queenly* name. Don't you know?'

Rattu didn't like people laughing at her. She felt like stomping her feet again. 'That's not fair,' said Rattu. 'Nobody told me.'

'Now you can tell everybody,' said a small voice.

Rattu stood on her toes and stretched out her neck, and she saw a small boy sitting behind the first soldier, whose queenly name was Lakshmi Bai.

'Who are you?' said Rattu.

'My name is Damodar Rao,' said the boy.

'Hello, Damodar Rao,' said Rattu. 'Do you know how to ride a horse?'

'Yes,' said Damodar Rao.

'Not yet,' said Lakshmi Bai.

'I bet *I* could ride a horse better than you,' said Rattu.

'I bet you couldn't,' said Damodar Rao.

'I bet I could,' said Rattu.

'I bet you couldn't,' said Damodar Rao.

'Stoppit,' said Jhalkari Bai and Lakshmi Bai. 'You wished for us, now tell us what you want.'

'Oh!' Rattu remembered. 'I want you to fight Poorie!'

'What's Poorie? Is it a company with guns and money?' asked Lakshmi Bai.

'No!'

'Is it a general with an army?' asked Jhalkari Bai.

'No!'

'Is it a monster with sharp teeth?' asked Damodar Rao.

'No!' said Rattu. 'Poorie is my sister. Don't you know?'

'Oh,' said everyone. 'Well, come along then. Where is she? Let's fight her.'

'Yay!' said Rattu, and she jumped from the bed on to Bijli's back.

Bijli and Badal turned around and trotted out of the bedroom, towards the balcony.

'Where are you going?' said Rattu. 'The front door is that way!'

But just as she said it, the horses went galloping off to the balcony and *leaped* right off it.

The horses and the two soldiers and Damodar Rao and Rattu fell a long and windy way through the air. They fell past trees and they fell past pigeons, and they fell past dishes meant for televisions. And when they had fallen as far as they could, they landed in the park down below.

'There!' shouted Rattu. 'There's Poorie!'

Poorie was playing with her friends. They were shooting arrows up in the air and running to catch them.

'Oh,' said Poorie when she saw the horses and the soldiers and Damodar Rao and Rattu. 'What's all this?'

'This is Lakshmi Bai and Jhalkari Bai and Badal and Bijli and Damodar Rao,' said Rattu. 'I bet you don't know who they are.'

'I bet I do,' said Poorie. 'Lakshmi Bai is the queenly name of the Rani of Jhansi, whose real name is Manikarnika. I read about her in my history book. She's very famous.'

'Thank you,' said Lakshmi Bai. 'I'm glad *someone* reads their history book.'

'But I never read about Jhalkari Bai,' said Poorie. 'She's not famous. Now go away, we're very busy.'

Jhalkari Bai turned to Rattu and said, 'Shall I chop her head off?'

Rattu thought about it. 'That would be very nice,' she said, 'but Mama and Papa will be *hopping mad* if you do.'

'Oh,' said Jhalkari Bai. 'Well, what do you want then?'

Rattu thought about it some more. She was in a park with a jungle gym and three swings and lots of grass and a slide. There were the soldiers and their horses and Damodar Rao and all of Poorie's friends.

'I want to play,' said Rattu, to all of them.

'Okay,' said Lakshmi Bai, 'do you want to play the Siege of Jhansi?'

'Yes!' said Rattu.

'Yes!' said Damodar Rao.

'That's stupid,' said Poorie. 'It's just a boring battle.'

'Oh, really?' said Lakshmi Bai, 'Well, when Jhalkari Bai and I were fighting in the battle of

Jhansi, we played a very clever trick that was not at all boring. But I suppose you know all about it?'

'Um,' said Poorie, 'what trick?'

'You don't know?' said Lakshmi Bai.

'No,' said Poorie, looking irritated.

'It wasn't in your history book?' said Jhalkari Bai, and she winked at Rattu.

'Fine,' said Poorie, 'you can all come and play with us, if you want.'

'They're *my* friends,' said Rattu. 'You have to ask me if you want to play with *my* friends.'

'You can have your bow-and-arrow   set back if you play with us,' said Poorie.

'Oh,'   said Rattu. 'Okay.'

'Come along, then,' said Lakshmi Bai and Jhalkari Bai. 'Come along and listen.'

And they told Rattu and Poorie and Damodar Rao and all of Poorie's friends . . .

The Story of the Game of
the Siege of Jhansi

Once upon a time, there was a town called Jhansi. Jhansi was full of all kinds of people. There were weavers who made cloth, and potters who made pots and farmers who grew all kinds of food in their farms. There were librarians who took care of books and there were actors and musicians who made stories and plays.

The biggest building in Jhansi was the fort. The fort was taller than any tree and harder than any rock.

The rani of the fort was called Lakshmi Bai. Rani Lakshmi Bai was married to an old king called Gangadhar Rao and they adopted a small boy called Damodar.

'That's me!' said Damodar Rao.

'That's right,' said Jhalkari Bai.

'You're adopted?' said Poorie.

'Yes,' said Lakshmi Bai. 'Now, let us finish.'

When the old king died, the rani went to the Company and said—

'What's the Company?' said Rattu.

'The Company had many soldiers and lots of money,' said Lakshmi Bai and Jhalkari Bai. 'And it always wanted more.'

So the rani said to the Company, 'Since Damodar is too small to be king just yet, I'll take care of things until he grows up.'

But the Company said, 'No. The fort is ours, you'll have to leave—we'll not ask twice, nor once say please!'

'But I am the rani!' said the rani. 'And Damodar is the new king. I will not leave Jhansi!'

'Too bad,' said the Company. 'We'll give you a pension—that's money, you'll need it. Off you go, chop-chop now, take it or leave it!'

The Company had so much money and so many soldiers that the rani had to leave the fort. All the rani's friends and soldiers went with her. Her bravest soldier was called Jhalkari Bai.

One day, Jhalkari Bai came running to the rani and said, 'Rani! Come quick! There's chaos, there's panic! The Company's soldiers are saying they've had it!'

'Had it?' said the rani. 'Had it with what?'

'They don't like the Company, they want you to be queen! They've captured the fort, now they're off to Delhi!'

Quickly, the rani and Jhalkari Bai jumped on their horses and galloped towards the Jhansi Fort. On the way, they saw a group of soldiers stomping their feet:

Down-down with the Company!
Up with the Mughal in Delhi!
Who wants to fight for the Company?
Not us! We're marching to Delhi!

'What's happening in Delhi?' said the rani.

'No time to find out!' said Jhalkari Bai. 'Let's get to the fort.'

When the rani and Jhalkari Bai reached the fort, they found all the weavers and potters and farmers and librarians and actors and musicians of Jhansi waiting for them. 'Rani, be our queen again!' said all the people of Jhansi. 'We don't want the Company.'

So, *the rani was queen of Jhansi for many months. But one day, Jhalkari Bai came running to the rani again and said, 'Rani! General Rose is coming with hundreds of soldiers, and he wants to capture our fort and kill everyone!'*

'Who's General Rose?' said Rattu.

'General Rose was a general in the army of the Company,' said Lakshmi Bai. 'And he was very angry.'

'Why?' said Poorie.

'Well,' said Jhalkari Bai, 'General Rose and the Company did not want the rani to be queen of Jhansi. And they were angry that the people of Jhansi liked the rani more than they liked the Company.'

When Jhalkari Bai told the rani that General Rose was coming to capture the fort and kill everyone, the rani said, 'Then we have to fight him off,' and she told all her soldiers to get ready for a big battle.

The next day, General Rose stood outside Jhansi with his army and shouted, 'Come out, Rani, let the Company back in! If you don't, we will fight you. Watch out, we're coming!'

But the rani was clever. 'I've locked all the gates,' she said. 'Ha-ha! You can't come in!'

'Then we'll fight you from outside!' said General Rose, and all his soldiers took out their cannonballs and guns.

'Fire!' shouted General Rose.

'Fire!' shouted the rani.

Bullets banged and cannons boomed and fire whizzed through the air!

And with every boom and bang and whizz, the general shouted, 'Take that, Rani!' and the rani shouted, 'Take that, you Rose!'

This went on for many days, until the battlefield began to look like . . .

a smashed-up doll and . . .

a squished-up cake and . . .

a bed Rattu had stomped.

As long as the gates of Jhansi were locked, General Rose could never come in. But then, one day, Jhalkari Bai ran to the rani and said, 'The gates are locked but a wall has been broken! The general is coming in!'

'Let's go and throw him out!' said the rani.

'Yes!' said Jhalkari Bai.

The rani and Jhalkari Bai and all the rani's soldiers ran out to fight General Rose. But after they had fought for many hours, Jhalkari Bai turned to the rani and said, 'I think you should run out and get help from our friends. I'll stay here and fight General Rose.'

'But if I run away, General Rose will think I'm scared!'

'No,' said Jhalkari Bai, 'he won't even know you've run away. Nobody will know.'

'How's that?' said the rani.

'Just look,' said Jhalkari Bai, and she pulled out a mirror from her pocket. 'See? We look exactly the same! I'll wear your clothes and pretend to be you, and General Rose will get properly fooled!'

'Ha-ha, you're right!' said the rani. Quickly, she picked up Damodar Rao, jumped up on Badal and leaped off the walls of the fort.

The rani and Damodar Rao and Badal fell like raindrops through the smoky, rainy, stomped-on air. They fell past cannonballs and they fell past arrows and they fell past bullets going bang!—until they landed on the ground. Then they ran.

And Jhalkari Bai put on the rani's clothes and galloped off to fight General Rose. And nobody knew that the rani had gone.

'Then what happened?' said Poorie.

'Well,' said Lakshmi Bai (which was the rani's queenly name), 'Jhalkari Bai was captured by General Rose.'

'Oh no!' said Rattu.

'Oh yes,' said Jhalkari Bai, 'but don't worry. You should have seen the look on his face when I told him that the real rani had run away. General Rose was properly fooled!'

'Was it a face like this?' said Rattu, and she made one of her best ghastly faces.

'A little bit,' said Lakshmi Bai. 'Now that we've told you the story, you can play.'

So Rattu and Poorie and Damodar Rao and all their friends ran to the jungle gym (which was also the fort), and they played the Siege of Jhansi for one hour and twenty-five minutes.

When it began to get dark, Jhalkari Bai said, 'It's time to go home.'

Rattu and Damodar Rao clambered on to Badal and Bijli's backs. Poorie looked as if she wished she could clamber on to a horse too.

'Shall we take Poorie with us?' asked Jhalkari Bai. 'Or are you still in a bad, mad mood?'

'We can take her,' said Rattu, who had played as much as she wanted, and no longer felt like making ghastly faces or stomping her feet.

As the horses carried the soldiers, the two sisters and Damodar Rao back home, Rattu said, 'Did you fight *many* wars?'

'Yes,' said Lakshmi Bai, 'lots.'

'Did you win *all* of them?' asked Poorie.

'Nobody can win *all* wars,' said Jhalkari Bai.

'I bet I could,' said Damodar Rao.

'I bet I could *too*,' said Rattu.

'I bet I could *three*,' said Poorie.

'Okay,' said Lakshmi Bai and Jhalkari Bai. 'But now it's time to sleep.'

Just as they said it, they reached Rattu and Poorie's bedroom. Poorie was so sleepy, she didn't even notice her bed was a crumpled, chewed-up, doggy-muddy mess. Rattu was so sleepy, she climbed into Poorie's bed and fell asleep next to her. Damodar Rao was so sleepy, he crawled into his mother's lap and closed his eyes.

As Rattu and Poorie and Damodar Rao fell fast asleep, Lakshmi Bai and Jhalkari Bai kissed each one of them, and whispered, 'Goodnight.'

Then they patted their horses' heads and whispered, 'Goodnight,' to them too.

And then Lakshmi Bai and Jhalkari Bai closed their own eyes, and fell asleep on their horses, like soldiers sometimes do.

NANA SAHIB AND AZIMULLAH KHAN

Rattu woke up one morning in the usual way. At first she was all fuzzy. Her eyes were awake but her head was asleep. She yawned, and Mama gave her a kiss.

'Wake up,' said Mama. 'It's a special day.'

'Oh!' said Rattu. Her sleepy head woke up. It was Poorie's birthday!

Rattu liked birthdays; they put her in a happy, clappy mood. Rattu's own birthday was her favourite day, but Poorie's birthday was her second favourite. On Poorie's birthday, they would have Poorie's favourite breakfast: chicken wings with idlis and chocolate milk. Later, in school, Poorie would get ice-cream for everyone in her class.

Even though Rattu was not in her class, Poorie would get ice-cream for her too. After school, Poorie's friends would come home with presents and they would eat cake with chips, and drink orange juice. Rattu would play with Poorie and all her friends until it was time to sleep.

When everyone had left, Rattu and Poorie, Mama and Papa and Roundy the cat would all sit on Poorie's bed and open all her presents. Rattu liked Poorie's presents even more than she liked her own. When Poorie got a book, she would let Rattu read it second. When Poorie got a toy, she would let Rattu hold it (for a minute).

After all the presents were opened, Rattu would give Poorie *her* present. Last year, Rattu had given Poorie a very white rock from the playground. This year, she would give her something even better.

'Hurry up!' shouted Poorie. 'Hurry up, or the ice-cream will melt!'

Poorie and her friends were walking into the school canteen and Rattu was running behind them.

'I'm coming,' Rattu shouted. 'Wait for me!'

Inside the canteen, the ice-cream man was waiting for them.

'What will you have?' asked the ice-cream man. 'Chocolate-banana? Strawberry is nice. Vanilla is delicious and very well priced! What about blackberry? Or apricot and cherry? Or would you like a frozen cone that's full of melted ice?'

'No,' said Poorie. 'We don't want to eat melted ice.'

'That's all right,' said the ice-cream man. 'Look, here's the cone in my left hand! I'll fill it up with pista-green, now here's a scoop of tangerine. Add a scoop of apple-red? Oh no, here's jamun-blue instead! Would you like to end with fudge? Is that too much? Or not enough? Oops, the scoops are piling higher! Here's your cone to gobble up.'

The ice-cream man's hands flew left and right and up and down, and before anyone knew what was what, Rattu and Poorie and all of Poorie's friends were holding tall and wobbly cones of ice-cream.

Rattu opened her mouth to take a bite, when—

'What's going on here?' said a big rude voice.

Rattu closed her mouth and looked around. A group of very big boys and girls was standing behind them.

'What's going on?' said the big rude voice again.

A very big girl grabbed the ice-cream cone from Rattu's hand. 'Look at all you greedy gluts,' said the very big girl in a very rude voice. 'I'm going to eat your ice-cream.'

'I am not a greedy glut!' said Rattu and she stomped her foot. 'Give it back!'

But the very big girl just laughed. All the other big boys and girls grabbed the ice-creams from Poorie and Poorie's friends and began to eat them.

'Goodbye, greedy gluts,' they said and went away.

'Catch them!' said Rattu. 'Poorie, they took all our ice-cream!'

Poorie made an angry face. 'I know,' she said. 'They're big bullies, and I hate them!'

'Let's catch them,' said Rattu.

Rattu and Poorie and all of Poorie's friends gave a big yell and began to run after the big bullies.

'Give us back our ice-cream!' they shouted. 'Give us back our cones!'

But when they reached the big bullies, it was too late. All the ice-cream was finished. 'Your ice-cream's in our tummies!' The big bullies laughed. 'Now go away.'

Rattu and Poorie and all of Poorie's friends went to a corner of the playground and they grumbled.

'Big bullies are mean.'

'Big bullies are rotten.'

'Big bullies are pimply.'

'Big bullies are *rude*.'

'They ate all our ice-cream and ruined our mood!'

After they had grumbled for a while, Rattu said, 'I wish there was someone who could get our ice-cream back.'

Just as Rattu made her wish, a big wind began to blow. And just as Rattu made her wish, the trees began to shake and a leaf fell on her nose.

'Oh!' thought Rattu. 'This leaf will be a nice present for Poorie.'

She put the leaf in her pocket. And just as she did, a man stood up in front of her. He had a big white turban on his head and a fluffy black beard all over his cheeks and chin. Between the turban and the beard, he had two dark eyes, a small nose and a big smile.

'Who are you?' said Rattu and Poorie and all of Poorie's friends.

'I am Azimullah Khan,' said the man with the turban and the fluffy beard. 'Who are *you*?'

When Rattu and Poorie and all of Poorie's friends had told him their names, Azimullah Khan made a little bow and said, '*On-chon-tay*!'

'On-chon-tay?' said Rattu. 'What does that mean?'

'It means I'm glad to meet you,' said Azimullah Khan. 'It's French.'

'You're not French,' said Poorie. 'French people don't wear turbans.'

'French people can wear turbans,' said Azimullah Khan. 'If they want to.'

'But they don't,' said Poorie.
'But they could,' said Azimullah Khan.
'But they won't,' said Poorie.
'But they might,' said Azimullah Khan.
'But they shan't,' said Poorie.
'But they should and they would—if they could, am I right? Wouldn't you if you could when it's cold in the night?'
'Oh,' said Poorie.

'Now,' said Azimullah Khan, 'why do you look like you've all caught the grumps?'

Rattu and Poorie and all of Poorie's friends told Azimullah Khan what had happened.

'Aha!' said Azimullah Khan when they had finished. 'Ate up all your ice-cream, I see! Without so much as a by-your-leave! Well, don't you worry. I know how to deal with big bullies.'

'Are you a soldier?' said Rattu.

'No,' said Azimullah Khan. 'I am a diwan.'

'Is that another French word?' said Poorie.

'Certainly not,' said Azimullah Khan. 'It is a Persian word.'

'What does it mean?' said Rattu.

'It means that I am a man who makes plans,' said Azimullah Khan and he tapped his turban with a finger.

'Oh, really?' said Poorie. 'What kind of plans?'

'What kind of plans, you ask? What kind of plans, indeed! Have you not read all about me in your history books?'

'No,' said Poorie.

Azimullah Khan looked a little sad. Rattu felt sorry for him and patted his arm.

'Don't worry,' said Rattu. 'She didn't know about Jhalkari Bai either.'

'I see,' said Azimullah Khan, and he cheered up. 'Well, I hope you know about Nana Sahib.'

'Yes, we do,' said Poorie and all of Poorie's friends. 'He's in our history book.'

'History book?' said Azimullah Khan. 'Not at all—he's right behind you!'

And just as he said it, his eyes began to glow and his nose began to twitch. Rattu and Poorie and all of Poorie's friends turned around and saw a man with a round face standing behind them. He was wearing an orange turban on top of his head and a curly moustache under his nose.

Nana Sahib looked at all the children and said, 'Hello. What's going on here?'

'I was telling them about plans,' said Azimullah Khan.

'Aha!' said Nana Sahib as he looked around at Rattu and Poorie and all of Poorie's friends. 'My friend and diwan Azimullah Khan made a plan to make me peshwa again.'

'What's a peshwa?' said Rattu.

'A peshwa is like a king,' said Nana Sahib.

'Why did you stop being king?' said Poorie.

'Well,' said Nana Sahib, 'how could I be king without a kingdom?'

'What happened to your kingdom?' said all of Poorie's friends.

'Some big bullies took it away,' said Nana Sahib and he made a face.

'Oh!' said Rattu and Poorie and all of Poorie's friends. 'That's what happened to us!'

'Is that so?' said Nana Sahib. 'Well, why don't you sit down and we'll tell you our story.'

The Story of Nana Sahib, Azimullah Khan and the Big Bullies

Once upon a time, Nana Sahib lived in the palace of Bithoor. Bithoor was a little town by the side of a big river called the Ganga, and Nana Sahib's palace was very large and very comfortable, but Nana Sahib wasn't happy.

Nana Sahib's father was the peshwa of the Marathas. Once upon a time, the empire of the Marathas was so great and so big that you could walk all day and all night for days and weeks and still not reach the end of it. But then, as time passed, the empire became smaller and weaker, until, one day, a company of big bullies came to Nana Sahib's father and said, 'You don't need an empire any more. Give it to us and go away.'

'Was it the same Company that took Jhansi from the rani?' said Rattu.

'The very same,' said Azimullah Khan.

Now, Nana Sahib's father tried to fight the Company, but he lost. 'You will be the last peshwa,' said the Company. 'Go away and take this pension—that's money—so you can buy the things you need.'

The last peshwa lived in Bithoor for many years, until he grew very old and then he died. Now it was Nana Sahib's turn to become peshwa, but the Company said, 'No. The last peshwa has gone and no more shall there be!'

'But what about the pension?' said Nana Sahib.

'Didn't you hear?' said the Company. 'The pension is only for the peshwa, and you are not the peshwa, are you?'

'But I am!' said Nana Sahib. 'My father was the peshwa. And my father's father was the peshwa. And my father's father's father was the peshwa! I am the peshwa too.'

'No,' said the Company. 'Certainly not. You are adopted, are you not?'

'Yes, *but so what?*' said Nana Sahib. '*I am the peshwa, can't you see?*'

But the Company would not listen. All it would say is 'The last peshwa has gone and no more shall there be!'

'*Was Nana Sahib adopted like Damodar Rao?*' said Poorie.

'*Exactly,*' said Nana Sahib. '*Now listen . . .*'

Nana Sahib and Azimullah Khan walked up and down the palace of Bithoor, trying to think of a plan.

'*The Company will not listen . . .*'

'*The Company doesn't care!*'

'*The Company's a nuisance . . .*'

'*The Company's annoying!*'

'*I'd like to take the Company . . .*'

'*And throw it far from here!*'

They thought like this for many days and many nights until finally Nana Sahib twirled his moustache and said, 'I wish we could talk to the London Queen.'

'*The London Queen?*' *said Azimullah Khan.* '*How can she help us?*'

'Well,' said Nana Sahib, 'the Company won't listen to anyone except the London Queen. If she tells the Company that I am the peshwa, the Company will have to agree.'

'Aha!' said Azimullah Khan. 'Then what are we waiting for? I will go to London in the morning!'

Azimullah galloped from Bithoor towards the salty sea. He got on a ship and sailed for many weeks until he reached the faraway city of the London Queen.

'Now,' thought Azimullah Khan, as he carried his luggage into his new flat on Upper George Street, 'who will take me to the queen?'

It is hard, as you know, to meet a queen without an appointment. It is also hard to get an appointment without an introduction. And it is very hard to get an introduction without a friend.

Luckily for Azimullah Khan, he made a good friend in London. His friend was called Lady Lucie. Lady Lucie wore a hat full of flowers on her head and she introduced Azimullah Khan to many people.

She introduced him to her mother and father, who gave Azimullah Khan many oranges to eat. She introduced him to William Thackeray and Charles Dickens, who told Azimullah Khan all about the books they had written. Azimullah Khan enjoyed meeting these people, but the one person he really wanted to meet was the London Queen.

Azimullah Khan went to Lady Lucie and said, 'Lady Lucie, Lady Lucie, take me to the queen! I've seen the Thames, I've heard Big Ben, I've met Browning and Tennyson—but what I want to do most now is meet the London Queen!'

'All right,' said Lady Lucie. 'I'll take you on Tuesday.'

On Tuesday, Lady Lucie and Azimullah Khan went to the great big palace where the London Queen lived.

The London Queen had big diamonds around her neck and a shiny crown on her head. Azimullah Khan went up to her and bowed. 'Hello, Queen,' he said. 'Would you please tell the Company that Nana Sahib is the peshwa?'

The London Queen tilted her head this way and that as she thought about it. Then she said, 'No. I'm

afraid I cannot do that, Azimullah Khan. But I will write a letter to Nana Sahib, so that we can be friends.'

The London Queen clapped her hands and a man brought out a table, and a second man brought out a sheet of paper, and a third man brought out a ruler, and a fourth man came running behind them all with a fat fountain pen. The London Queen put the paper on the table and drew margins with the ruler and wrote a letter with the pen. Then she looked up at the four men. 'Ahem,' she said. 'None of you remembered to bring me an envelope!'

At this, the four men jumped in alarm and scurried off in four different directions. The London Queen made a gloomy face.

'Don't worry, Queen,' said Lady Lucie. 'I have a nice envelope here, in my purse.'

'Thank you,' said the London Queen. She put her letter in Lady Lucie's nice envelope and gave it to Azimullah Khan.

But Azimullah Khan wasn't happy. 'I came to get a pension for the peshwa,' he grumbled to Lady Lucie, 'and all I got was a letter!'

Lady Lucie tried to cheer him up, but Azimullah Khan grew more grumpy every day, until finally he declared, 'I am going back to Bithoor.'

And just like that, he took all his luggage from Upper George Street and got on a ship and sailed back home.

As soon as he saw Azimullah Khan, Nana Sahib shouted, 'You're back! Just in time.'

'I met the queen,' said Azimullah Khan. 'She's sent a letter for you.'

'Well,' said Nana Sahib, 'letters are nice, but now's not the time. Do you know, since you left, there has been an uproar? A clamour, a rumpus, and havoc galore?'

'What's happened?' said Azimullah Khan.

'The Company's in trouble! It's got a big fright.'

'I don't understand,' said Azimullah Khan.

'Oh, listen. The soldiers who fought for the Company have said they will not any more. And listen to this—without soldiers, the Company cannot tell us what to do!'

'Oh!' Azimullah Khan dropped all his luggage on the floor. 'Now I understand. Hurry, let us go and find these soldiers.'

Nana Sahib and Azimullah Khan got on their horses and galloped out of the palace of Bithoor. When they had galloped for a little while, they saw a large group of soldiers marching in a dusty way and singing a lusty song:

Down-down with the Company!
Up with the Mughal in Delhi!
Who wants to fight for the Company?
Not us! We're marching to Delhi!

'Hang on, hang on,' said Azimullah Khan. 'Why are you marching to Delhi?'

'We're off to meet the Mughal badshah,' said the soldiers. 'We will make him emperor of India and get rid of the Company!'

'Hang on, hang on,' said Azimullah Khan. 'The Company has so many soldiers in so many places. Are they all marching to Delhi?'

'Yes, they are,' said the soldiers. 'And so are we!'

'Now, wait a minute,' said Azimullah Khan. 'It looks to me like the Mughal badshah will have enough soldiers and more to help him. But you are soldiers of Bithoor. Have you forgotten all about your peshwa Nana Sahib?'

'That's right,' said Nana Sahib. 'The Company has bullied us long enough. Come with me, and we shall teach them a lesson and I shall be your peshwa again!'

The soldiers looked at each other and thought about it. 'You're right,' they said and they turned around and began to sing a different song:

Down-down with the Company!
Nana Sahib will the peshwa be!
Who wants to fight for the Company?
Not us! We'll fight for our Nanaji!

'Then what happened?' said Poorie.

'Well,' said Nana Sahib.

'Well,' said Azimullah Khan.

'Well what?' said Rattu.

'There was a lot of fighting,' said Nana Sahib.

'And did you become peshwa again?' said Rattu and Poorie and all of Poorie's friends.

'Just for a little while,' said Nana Sahib.

'But who won the fighting?' said Rattu.

'Well,' said Azimullah Khan, 'for a while, we did.'

'And then,' said Nana Sahib, 'the Company did.'

'So you lost,' said Poorie.

'Well,' said Nana Sahib, 'that's one way of putting it.'

'Another way,' said Azimullah Khan, 'would be to say we tried.'

'Trying is not the same as winning,' said Poorie.

'Maybe not,' said Azimullah Khan. 'But if some big bullies took your ice-cream, wouldn't you want to try and get it back?'

Poorie thought about it. 'I suppose so,' she said.

'But they've eaten it all up!' said Rattu.

'Come along,' said Nana Sahib and Azimullah Khan. 'Let's see what we can do.'

Nana Sahib and Azimullah Khan and Rattu and Poorie and all of Poorie's friends went marching up to the big bullies. 'Give us back our ice-cream now! Give it back or, big bullies, we'll jump on you like chimpanzees!'

But the big bullies just laughed and said, 'Who do you think you are?'

'Well,' said Nana Sahib, 'I am the son of the last peshwa.'

'And I am his diwan,' said Azimullah Khan.

'Whatever,' said the big bullies. 'The ice-cream is in our tummies.'

'Hang on, hang on,' said Azimullah Khan. 'Has the ice-cream man run out of ice-cream?'

'No,' said the big bullies.

'Well,' said Nana Sahib, 'has the ice-cream man left the canteen?'

'No,' said the big bullies.

'Well, then,' said Nana Sahib and Azimullah

Khan, 'kindly get ice-creams for Rattu and Poorie and all of Poorie's friends!'

'No,' said the big bullies. 'We don't want to.'

At this, Nana Sahib's and Azimullah Khan's eyes began to glow and their noses began to twitch. 'Oh,' they said, 'but you *do* and you shall and you will and you *must*—or all the sweets that you eat from now on shall be dust!'

'Oh,' said the big bullies, and they looked worried.

'That's right,' said Nana Sahib and Azimullah Khan, and their eyes shone bright. 'The next time you bite into chocolate cake? Oh gosh, oh boy, what a shock you will get! Will it be gooey and warm? You would think so, but no! It will taste of karela boiled up with black mould! Your sweets will be glue, your treats will be rubber. When you next have dessert, you'll taste an old scrubber!'

'Oh,' said the big bullies, and they looked even more worried.

'Now, then,' said Nana Sahib and Azimullah Khan, 'kindly look lively and get us our treats!'

The big bullies jumped in the air and ran to the ice-cream man, and they brought back all the ice-creams that they had taken from Rattu and Poorie and all of Poorie's friends. And they brought two extra ones too, for Nana Sahib and Azimullah Khan.

Everyone ate their ice-creams until the bell rang. Then Rattu and Poorie and all of Poorie's friends ran back to their classrooms. Nana Sahib and Azimullah Khan waved goodbye to the children, and they walked across the playground and out of the gate . . . and into thin air.

BAHADUR SHAH ZAFAR

'Off and out and up and go!' said Papa at the door. This is what he liked to say when he was ready and everyone else was not.

Mama picked up Rattu's water bottle in one hand and Poorie's shoes in the other. 'Keep your hair on!' she said. This is what she liked to say when Papa shouted from the door.

'My hair is stuck!' said Rattu. This is what she liked to say when Mama told Papa to keep his hair on. It made Rattu wonder if her own hair would come off, like a hat. But it never did.

'That's just as well,' said Mama, and she took out a comb and a handkerchief, four almonds and two earrings from her pockets. She put on the earrings and picked up a bag full of Rattu and Poorie's clothes and toys. 'Are you ready?' said Mama.

Poorie picked up her book and Rattu picked up Roundy the cat. 'Yes!' they said.

Mama and Papa and Rattu and Poorie and Roundy the cat went out of the front door and into their red car, and they drove to Ajju's house.

Ajju was Rattu and Poorie's Mama's Papa. He lived in a crumbly house with a big garden and lots of bees. Besides the bees, Ajju had two cows, three goats and eight chickens, as well as a big pond full of fish. Ajju also had a parrot called Badshah. Badshah was as white as Ajju's beard and he liked to say, 'Soupy!'

'Does Badshah like soup?' said Rattu to Ajju.

'Soup is not for parrots, unless it's made with carrots,' said Ajju.

And that was that.

Whenever Mama spoke to Ajju on her phone screen, she said, 'You can't just live with bees and cows and goats and chickens and a parrot! You're getting old. Come and live with us at home.'

'Speak for yourself!' said Ajju. 'I'm as young as the Himalayas!'

'That's just silly,' said Mama. 'The Himalayas are mountains!'

'The Himalayas are as white as my beard,' said Ajju. 'And they are the youngest mountains in the world.'

'Uff!' said Mama, and she switched off the screen.

Rattu and Poorie did not think that Ajju was old. He could get milk from a cow and eggs from a chicken. He could catch a fish and he could light a fire. He could carry Rattu and Poorie, one by one, on his shoulders, when they wanted to be as tall as the Himalayas.

But this time, he was different.

Mama and Papa and Rattu and Poorie and Roundy the cat reached Ajju's crumbly old house, and Rattu ran inside. 'Come, Ajju, come!' she said. 'Let's play with the goats!'

'Shh!' said Mama. 'Ajju's resting.'

Ajju was in his bedroom and the curtains were drawn, so it was dark.

'Ajju?' said Rattu and Poorie together.

'Harrumph!' came a sound from the bed.

Mama went to the windows and parted the curtains.

'Soupy!' said Badshah as the light came in.

Ajju was lying on his bed. He was wearing a green kurta–pyjama and a grumpy face.

'Were you sleeping, Ajju?' said Poorie.

'No,' said Ajju.

'Were you dreaming, Ajju?' said Rattu.

'No,' said Ajju.

'Were you grumping?' said Mama.

Ajju gave her a grumpy look and said nothing.

Mama sat on Ajju's bed and gave him a kiss.

'Ajju is grumpy,' said Mama, 'because he has to leave this house.'

'Oh,' said Rattu. 'Will you take the goats with you?'

'No,' said Ajju, grumpily.

'Oh,' said Poorie. 'Will you take the chickens with you?'

'No,' said Ajju, gloomily. 'And not the cows nor the bees either, before you ask.'

'Why do you have to leave?' said Rattu and Poorie.

'Harrumph,' said Ajju, dolefully.

'Ajju has to leave so he can come and stay with us,' said Mama. 'And then we can take care of him properly.'

'Can't we take care of him properly here?' said Poorie.

'We could,' said Mama. 'But here is far away from my office and your school.'

'I don't mind being far away from my school,' said Rattu.

'But I do,' said Mama. 'Now, why don't the two of you sit with Ajju? I'm going to help Papa make lunch.'

Mama left the bedroom, and Rattu and Poorie climbed into Ajju's bed with him. Roundy the cat sat on the floor and blinked his eyes at Badshah.

'Soupy!' said Badshah, and hopped on to Ajju's shoulder.

'Your cat,' said Ajju, 'wants to eat up my parrot.'

'Oh no,' said Poorie. 'When a cat blinks its eyes, it means it wants to make friends.'

'Tell that to the parrot,' said Ajju.

'Don't worry, Badshah,' Rattu told the parrot. 'Roundy just wants to be your friend!'

'Soupy!' said Badshah, but he did not look happy about it.

'Why don't you want to come home with us, Ajju?' said Rattu and Poorie.

'Oh!' said Ajju. He gave Poorie a kiss and he gave Rattu a tickle. 'I do want to come with you. I just don't want to leave my home. Do you understand?'

'But then,' said Rattu, 'how will we take care of you properly?'

'I want to take care of myself!' said Ajju.

'I can't take care of myself,' said Rattu. 'At least not every part.'

'I can take care of myself,' said Poorie.

'No, you can't,' said Rattu.

'Yes, I can,' said Poorie.

'No, you can't,' said Rattu.

'Yes, I can,' said Poorie.

'Stoppit,' said Ajju. 'Nobody can take care of themselves all alone.'

'Not even grown-ups?' said Poorie.

'Not even grown-ups,' said Ajju.

'Not even grown-ups like you?' said Poorie.

'Well, yes,' said Ajju. 'Not even grown-ups like me.'

'Who takes care of grown-ups?' said Rattu.

Ajju thought about it for a minute. 'Friends take care of grown-ups,' he said.

'Don't you have friends, Ajju?' said Poorie.

Ajju thought about it for another minute. 'No,' he said, and began to look even more grumpy than before.

'I wish,' said Rattu, 'I wish Ajju had a friend to take care of him.'

And just as Rattu made her wish, the bed began to rattle and a cock began to crow. And just as Rattu made her wish, the lights began to flicker and a cow began to low.

'Moo,' said the cow.

And just as she said it, a very thin and dark and tired old man lay down in the bed next to Ajju. He had a beard that was as white as Ajju's, and no hair on his head.

'Did you take your hair off?' said Rattu. She pulled at her own hair, but it was still stuck.

'No,' said the thin and dark and tired old man. 'It went away on its own.'

'Who are you?' said Poorie.

'I am the badshah,' said the thin and dark and tired old man.

'No, you're not,' said Poorie, and she pointed at Ajju's parrot. '*That* is Badshah.'

'That may be, and well enough,' said the thin and dark and tired old man. 'But I am the Mughal badshah. I am Bahadur Shah the Second, and you may call me Zafar.'

'Oh,' said Poorie, 'I read about you in my history book.'

'Yes,' said Zafar, but he did not look happy about it.

'You're the last Mughal,' said Poorie.

'That's right,' said Zafar.

'Oh,' said Rattu, 'does that mean your father was a Mughal and your father's father was a Mughal and your father's father's father was a Mughal too?'

'Yes,' said Zafar. 'And many more before them.'

'Who was the first Mughal?' said Rattu.

'The very first?' said Zafar.

'Yes,' said Rattu and Poorie.

'The very first Mughal was called Babur.'

'Who was Babur?' said Rattu.

'Wait,' said Zafar. 'Let me gather my thoughts.'

Rattu and Poorie and Ajju waited as Zafar stroked his white beard and gathered his thoughts.

'Babur,' said Zafar, 'was an Uzbek prince.'

'Oh,' said Rattu and Poorie.

Zafar stroked his beard again and continued:

Babur was an Uzbek prince
Who wanted very much
To be the king of Samarkand
And eat melons for lunch.

But though he did, three times at least,
Begin to rule that city,
Each time he found himself kicked out,
Which was, he thought, a pity.

'Oh,' said Rattu and Poorie. 'So what did he do?'

'I know!' said Ajju, and he sat up in bed and stroked his own beard. 'I know this part. Babur decided he would be king of Hindustan instead. So he fought a big battle with Ibrahim Lodi in Panipat.'

They charged forth, did Babur's men,
All waving swords a-gleam, a-glint,
The other lot were led by Lodi
And harrumphing elephants.

But Babur had what Lodi hadn't:
Cannonballs and guns
That boomed and blasted, dawn to noon,
Until Babur had won.

'Was he glad he won?' said Rattu and Poorie.

'Of course!' said Zafar and Ajju. 'Babur was glad and so were his soldiers. "Yippee!" they said, "Hip-hip hooray!" And off they went to celebrate.'

They galloped all the way to Delhi
(Their hearts were full, their feet were smelly)
And when they reached, they shouted out,
'Take us to Lodi's palace now
And let us stomp and romp about,
And chomp on cake and sizzled trout!'

'Oh!' said Rattu. 'Like the trout in your pond, Ajju?'

'That's right,' said Ajju.

A grand old feast it was for sure,
With chicken wings and sweets galore,
With mangoes ripe as golden sun,
And boiled eggs cooked to perfection.

(To boil an egg, have this by rote:
Unless you like yours runny,
First boil the water, then the egg,
Eight minutes long, no more nor less,
Now let it cool—count to fifteen—
Tap the shell and peel it clean
And quickly transfer egg to tummy.)

'Raw eggs are yucky,' said Poorie.

'I agree,' said Zafar.

'What happened after Babur's party?' said Rattu. 'Did he get presents?'

'No,' said Zafar. 'But he did get a shock.'

'Oh,' said Rattu and Poorie, 'what happened?'

'Well . . .' said Zafar.

As Babur and his men they danced
About the palace corridors
They did not notice, as they pranced,
How Buwa sat apart and low.

'Who's Buwa?' said Rattu.

'Do you remember Ibrahim Lodi?' said Zafar. 'He lost the battle against Babur and his men.'

'Yes,' said Poorie.

'Well,' said Zafar, 'Buwa was Ibrahim Lodi's mother.'

Buwa, she was Lodi's mother,
And she was hopping mad!
And furious and aggravated,
Livid, cross, exasperated,
In a frenzy, inundated
With black thoughts she was.
As stated: Buwa wasn't glad.

'Why not?' said Rattu.

'Well,' said Ajju, 'wouldn't you be grumpy if you lost a battle?'

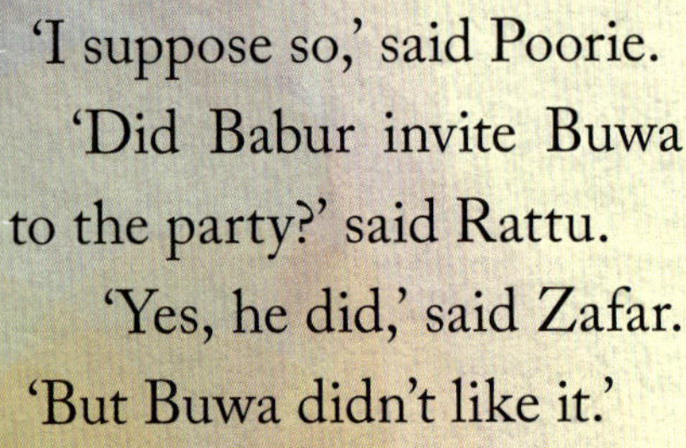

'I suppose so,' said Poorie. 'Did Babur invite Buwa to the party?' said Rattu. 'Yes, he did,' said Zafar. 'But Buwa didn't like it.'

How could these tall and
laughing fellows
Drink and dine and thump
and bellow?
Why, wasn't it quite bad
enough
To blow her son's one head
clean off?

'With a cannonball!' said Rattu.

'That's right,' said Zafar. 'Not much fun for Ibrahim Lodi.'

So she thought, and who could blame her
As she scurried to the kitchen,
Nudged the cook and whispered, 'Listen!
Take this arsenic and take

This venom glowing green,
Grind them both into a paste
And spike Babur's protein!'

'Did Buwa want to poison Babur?' said Poorie.

'Yes,' said Ajju. 'She wanted to bump him off. But the poor old cook, he wasn't keen to make the new king sick.'

'Did he say no to Buwa?' said Rattu.

'You don't say no to queens, oh no!' said Zafar. 'You say yes, double-quick.'

The cook, he went a-sprinkling
Her poison in a special stew
Of meat and raisins bubbling
In gravy spiced, and sweetish too.

And as he sprinkled, Buwa sang,
'Babur, prepare to meet your fate,
Babur, the dawn you shall not greet!
Oh, how I'll gloat and grin with glee!
Babur, Babur, bon appétit!'

'What's bon appétit?' said Poorie.

'It's French,' said Ajju. 'It means "Have a nice meal".'

'But poison isn't a nice meal,' said Rattu.

'Not at all,' said Ajju. 'That was Buwa's little joke.'

'So did Babur get bumped off?' said Poorie.

'Well,' said Zafar, 'almost . . . As soon as Babur tried the dish, his stomach churned and turned and squished. His liver lurched, his kidneys wobbled. "My lord," said Buwa, "you look troubled!"'

With a yowl and a yelp,
the king arose
And ran towards the
bathroom door,
But halfway there,
he stopped, he froze
And threw up on
the floor.

'Oh no,' said Rattu and Poorie.

'Oh yes,' said Zafar. 'As Babur lay upon the floor, a little dog came trotting by. He sniffed the vomit once or twice and thought, "Oh, that smells very nice!"'

'Yuckypoo!' said Rattu and Poorie. 'Who likes vomit?'

'Dogs do,' said Ajju. 'Not only did he sniff it, he ate it too! Yuckypoo!'

'Dogs don't have refined taste,' said Zafar.

Roundy the cat looked at them as if he agreed.

'Do cats have refined taste?' said Rattu.

'Your cat,' said Ajju, 'had better refine its taste away from my parrot!'

'Don't you want to know what happened to the dog?' said Zafar.

'Yes,' said Rattu and Poorie.

'Well,' said Zafar, 'sure enough, he, too, fell sick!'

Said Babur, 'It's a nasty trick,
Someone's played on us, my friend,
And when I find out who it was
They'll meet a grim and gory end.'

'Did Buwa get caught?' said Rattu.

'Well,' said Ajju, 'first it was the cook they caught. They tied him up and said, "Tell us what you know, and quick! Who put the poison in the stew? Was it you? Was it you?" They asked him once, they asked him twice . . .'

And in the end, he cried aloud,
'I'm just the cook, I am not proud
Of what I did—she made me do it,

Gave me venom, made me brew it.
Mine was the hand, Buwa's the brain!'

So Buwa, too, was put in chains.

'Oh no,' said Poorie. 'Did she meet a gory end?'

'Not exactly,' said Zafar. 'When Babur heard what the queen had done, he said, "Please leave the city. Each time I dine, I cannot form a vigilance committee!" So Buwa packed and went away. But the poor old cook . . .'

'Did he meet a gory end?' said Rattu.

'I'm afraid he did,' said Ajju.

But poor old cook was not let loose,
You might say Babur cooked his goose.
Which forms a lesson for us all:
Be born a queen, or not at all.

When this was done did Babur sigh
And pat the pup and mutter,
'Winning battles is great fun,
Parties, of course, are nice,
But kings whose foes want them undone
Are living a dog's life!'

'Poor cook,' said Poorie.

'Yes,' said Zafar.

'It wasn't really his fault,' said Rattu.

'Babur was angry,' said Ajju. 'Anger makes you take bad decisions.'

'Once I stomped on Poorie's bed,' said Rattu.

'Oh, I see,' said Zafar. 'Did you take your shoes off?'

'No,' said Rattu. 'I made a muddy mess.'

'Well,' said Zafar, 'better stomp on beds than heads!'

'Did you make bad decisions?' said Poorie.

'I suppose I did,' said Zafar. 'And I certainly had my share of foes!'

'Was Buwa your foe too?' said Rattu.

'No, silly!' said Poorie. 'Buwa was the foe of the first Mughal. Zafar is the last, don't you remember?'

'I'm not silly, you're silly!' said Rattu. She tried to stomp her feet but Ajju stopped her.

'Neither of you is silly,' said Ajju. 'Zafar's foe was much worse than Buwa.'

'That's right,' said Zafar, and he looked sad about it. 'My foe was the Company.'

'Oh!' said Rattu. 'Was it the same Company that fought with Lakshmi Bai and Jhalkari Bai?'

'Yes,' said Zafar.

'Oh!' said Poorie. 'Was it the same Company that fought with Nana Sahib and Azimullah Khan?'

'Yes,' said Zafar.

'Oh!' said Rattu. 'But all the soldiers of that Company got up and left.'

'Down-down with the Company!' sang Poorie.

'That's right,' said Zafar. 'The soldiers marched away.'

'Up with the Mughal in Delhi!' sang Rattu. Then she thought about it. 'Up where?'

'Well,' said Zafar, 'what the soldiers meant was: "Let's raise the Mughal badshah up against the Company!" And the Mughal badshah was me. But instead—'

'What?' said Poorie.

'But instead', said Zafar, 'it was the Company that pulled me down from my throne and made me leave my home.'

'Oh,' said Rattu.

'Oh,' said Poorie.

'Harrumph,' said Ajju.

'Did you have cows and goats and chickens in your home?' said Rattu. 'And a pond full of fish?'

'I had elephants,' said Zafar in a grand manner. 'And I had a river full of fish flowing by.'

'Did you have friends to take care of you properly?' said Poorie.

'Yes,' said Zafar. 'I had many friends, and we stayed up all night making poems.'

'Then why did you have to leave your home?' said Rattu and Poorie.

'Well,' said Zafar, stroking his beard, 'the Company came and fought us . . .'

'With cannonballs and guns?' said Rattu.

'Yes,' said Zafar.

'Did you fight back?' said Poorie. 'Like Nana Sahib and Azimullah Khan?'

'The soldiers fought back,' said Zafar, 'and my son the Mughal prince fought back. But I am old like Ajju and too old for fighting.'

'Did you play a trick on them,' said Rattu, 'like Laskhmi Bai and Jhalkari Bai?'

'Well,' said Zafar, 'I did try to run away. But I am old like Ajju and too old to run very far.'

'Did the Company catch you?' said Rattu and Poorie.

'The Company caught me,' said Zafar, and he sighed a very deep sigh. 'And the Company thought, "As long as the Mughal badshah remains in Delhi, more soldiers may come and raise him up again." So the Company sent me far away from my home and my elephants and my river full of fish—where no one could find me.'

'Harrumph,' said Ajju. 'The Company sounds a lot like Mama.'

Then Ajju told Zafar all about how Mama was taking him to live in her house without his cows or goats or chickens or bees.

'Harrumph,' said Zafar when Ajju had finished saying what he had to say. 'But your beard is as white as the Himalayas . . .'

'And they are the youngest mountains in the world. How right you are!' said Ajju, and he looked very pleased with himself.

Then Zafar and Ajju both stroked their beards and thought about things.

After a while, Zafar said, 'I would not have minded if the Company had sent me to live with Rattu and Poorie.'

'Of course not!' said Ajju. 'Rattu and Poorie are the best granddaughters an Ajju could have.'

'That's right,' said Zafar. 'But the Company put me in a cart and then on a boat and shut me in a hut in clammy Rangoon.'

'What's Rangoon?' asked Rattu.

'Rangoon is very far away,' said Zafar. 'Much farther away than your house.'

'You see, Ajju?' said Poorie. 'We're closer than Rangoon.'

'Well,' said Ajju, 'I suppose you are.'

'In Rangoon, no one could find me and I had nothing to do all day,' said Zafar.

'I'll take you to the park, Ajju,' said Rattu. 'You can play with all our friends.'

'Well,' said Ajju, 'I suppose I can.'

'In Rangoon, there was no one to make poems with,' said Zafar.

'Oh!' said Rattu. 'I'll make poems with you, Ajju. Do you want to hear my poem about Roundy and Badshah?'

'Well,' said Ajju, 'I suppose I do.'

Rattu recited her poem:

Roundy the cat
Won't eat Badshah
the parrot!'

That's not a poem,' said Poorie. 'Poems have to rhyme.'

'No, they don't,' said Rattu.

'Yes, they do,' said Poorie.

'No, they don't,' said Rattu.

'Stoppit,' said Ajju.

'Poems can be any way you want them to be,' said Zafar. 'As long as they make you happy.'

'And as long as they rhyme,' said Poorie.

'I bet,' said Rattu, licking her lips, 'I bet that I could make a hundred rhyming poems.'

'I bet you couldn't,' said Poorie.

'All right, let's try,' said Zafar:

We once had a ruby that weighed fifty carats.

'All right,' said Ajju, and replied:

We gave it away and we bought a white parrot.

'All right!' said Poorie:

When Roundy first heard

'All right!' said Rattu:

He tried to eat up the bird

'All right!' said all of them together:

So we sent him upstairs to catch mice in the garret!

'Ha-ha!' said Zafar and Ajju, and they stroked their beards, which were as white and as young as the Himalayas.

'Ha-ha,' said Rattu and Poorie, and they bounced on the bed, as if they were bouncing like fish in a lake.

'Ajju,' said Rattu when everyone had finished rhyming and bouncing, 'can Zafar come home with us too?'

'If he would like to,' said Ajju, and he looked quite happy about it.

'I would like to,' said Zafar. 'Your home sounds much nicer than my hut in Rangoon.'

'Good,' said Ajju. 'Now I'm ready for my nap.'

'Me too,' said Zafar.

Then Ajju and Zafar closed their eyes and fell asleep.

And Rattu and Poorie and Roundy the cat and Badshah the parrot went out of the room to see what Mama and Papa had made for lunch.

The Story of 1857

Before India was India, it was many other things, with many kinds of people and many kinds of queens and kings. There were the Mauryas, the Kushanas and the Guptas, the Pallavas, the Chalukyas and the Cholas. There were the rayas of Vijaynagar and the sultans of Ahmadnagar, the zamorins of Calicut, the ranas of Rajasthan and the maharajas of Punjab. There were the Mughal badshahs and the Maratha peshwas and the Awadhi nawabs.

And in the end, there was the British Raj.

The British Raj began with the East India Company, and the East India Company began with trade. Trade is what traders do when they buy and sell, and India has always been full of traders from around the world. There were traders from Rome and Arabia, Egypt and China, Turkey and Persia, and many other places.

The traders would sell what they had brought from Rome or China or Persia, and they would buy the things that were made or grown in India, like cloth and pepper and jewellery.

Whenever you have traders (and clothmakers and pepper farmers and jewellers), you also have to have rules—about prices and taxes and other such things. Rules are meant to make sure that everyone gets a fair deal. So all the many queens and kings of India made many rules, and all the many traders and clothmakers and pepper farmers and jewellers in India followed them.

But the Company was different.

At first, the Company was buying and selling like all the other traders, but then the Company decided that it didn't want to follow any rules. It wanted to make them.

If you want to make the rules, you must do one of two things: either you must make very fair deals so everyone trusts you, or you must be very scary so nobody questions you. The Company didn't care about fair deals. Instead, it got a lot of soldiers with a lot of guns so that people would be scared and would listen to all its rules.

One of the rules that the Company made was called the Doctrine of Lapse. According to the Doctrine of Lapse, if any king of India did not have a son, the Company would become king in his place.

This was the rule that the Company used when the king of Jhansi died. When Lakshmi Bai wanted Damodar Rao to be the new of king of Jhansi, the Company said, 'No. He's adopted. Haven't you heard of the Doctrine of Lapse?'

This was also the rule that the Company used when the last peshwa died. When Nana Sahib wanted to be the new peshwa of the Marathas, the Company said, 'No. You're adopted. Haven't you heard of the Doctrine of Lapse?'

Anyone can see that this was not a fair deal. Even so, the Company had so many soldiers with so many guns, that Lakshmi Bai and Nana Sahib had to listen.

But the Company forgot that soldiers like fair deals too. Instead, the Company was always ordering them to do things they didn't want to do. One day, the Company ordered them to use a new kind of gun with a new kind of bullet. Each bullet was wrapped in paper, and the wrapping was called the cartridge. When a soldier wanted to shoot, he would have to bite the cartridge, take out the bullet and put it into his gun.

Now, the problem was this: Each cartridge was dipped in grease, because grease helps to keep bullets dry—and if a bullet gets wet, you cannot shoot it. But grease doesn't taste very nice, and the soldiers didn't like biting into it. Besides, some people said, 'The grease comes from pigs!' And this made the Muslim soldiers angry, because many Muslims do not like to eat pigs. Other people said, 'The grease comes from cows!' And this made the Hindu soldiers angry, because many Hindus do not like to eat cows.

'What's in the grease?' said all the soldiers. 'Tell us!'

But the Company replied, 'Do as you're told!' And this made all the soldiers angry, because it isn't nice to be shouted at when all you want is an explanation.

So one day a soldier called Mangal Pandey said, 'No! I'll not work for the Company any more!' And one by one, many soldiers began to say, 'No! We'll not work for the Company any more!'

And the soldiers marched away from the Company, and as they marched away, they thought, 'The old kings were better than the Company. They knew how to make fair deals. Let's bring them back!'

Some soldiers decided they would help Lakshmi Bai become the rani of Jhansi. Some soldiers decided they would help Nana Sahib become the peshwa of the Marathas. And many soldiers decided they would make Bahadur Shah Zafar their leader. Bahadur Shah Zafar was too old to fight battles, but the soldiers made him their leader anyway, because he was the badshah of the Mughal empire, and the Mughal empire was one of the greatest empires of India and the world.

All of this happened in 1857, which is a date in history and also the name of this book.

History is full of dates, as you know. But what is more important than the dates is what happened on them. What happened in 1857 is called the Uprising.

In the Uprising of 1857, soldiers rose up to fight the Company, and many queens and kings joined them. They fought very hard, and many of them died, and all of them lost. But afterwards, the queen of England, who was called Victoria and lived in London, said to the Company, 'Nobody seems to like you very much. I don't think you should be making any more rules.'

So the Company went away, and Queen Victoria began to make rules for India. This was called the British Raj. The British Raj made all kinds of rules, all the way until 1947, which is another important date—and another story.

Acknowledgements

Thank you to all the people at Puffin India who've given Rattu and Poorie the benefit of their time and talent. I especially want to thank Hemali Sodhi and Sohini Mitra, who gave the book its form; Meghna Menon, who filled it with wonderful illustrations; and Smit Zaveri, who kept a close and kindly eye on its details, steering it through the many channels of edits, illustration and production with a steady hand.

Many thanks to Neelima Aryan and Parag Chitale for their work on the book's layout and design; and to Priya Doraswamy, my ever-encouraging agent.

Thanks also to Priyanka Malhotra and Puja Sood, with whom I worked on a draft of one of these stories.

Finally, I must acknowledge Tahseen and Shahrukh Alam for suffering nobly through my drafts, Fatima Alam for suffering me to produce them at a safe distance, and my younger sibling, Gayatri Sharma for suffering nobly at my hands for much of our childhood. I can only hope she never writes a history of her own.